The Voyages of Sindbad the Sailor

Level 2

Retold by Pauline Francis
Series Editors: Andy Hopkins and Jocelyn Potter

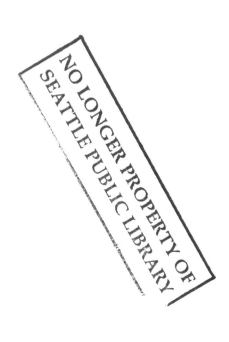

Pearson Education Limited
Edinburgh Gate, Harlow,
Essex CM20 2JE, England
and Associated Companies throughout the world.

ISBN: 978-1-4058-5542-6

First published by Penguin Books 2000
This edition published 2008

1 3 5 7 9 10 8 6 4 2

Text copyright © Penguin Books Ltd 2000
This edition copyright © Pearson Education Ltd 2008
Illustrations by Andrew Brown

Typeset by Graphicraft Ltd, Hong Kong
Set in 11/14pt Bembo
Printed in China
SWTC/01

Published by Pearson Education Ltd in association with
Penguin Books Ltd, both companies being subsidiaries of Pearson Plc

For a complete list of the titles available in the Penguin Readers series please write to your local
Pearson Longman office or to: Penguin Readers Marketing Department, Pearson Education,
Edinburgh Gate, Harlow, Essex CM20 2JE, England.

Contents

Introduction

It was a giant! He was very, very big. He was a man, but he was as tall as the tallest tree. His eyes were as red as fire. His mouth was as wide as a cave, and his teeth were as long as elephant tusks.

Sindbad the Sailor went to sea seven times and his voyages were always dangerous. He met giants – giant men, giant snakes and giant birds . . . and the Old Man of the Sea!

The Sindbad stories come from the *Arabian Nights* (or the *Thousand and One Nights* – or, in Arabic, *Alf Leila wa Leila*). People read the first book of the *Arabian Nights* in Arabic in about the year 940, or AH 330. We think that the Sindbad stories came after that.

At that time, Arab sailors sailed to countries a long way away. We know about the journeys and voyages of Suleiman al-Tajir (Suleiman the Merchant). He told people in Arab countries about China, India and South-East Asia.

Could Arab ships sail to China at that time? Yes. One man, Tim Severin, made the voyage in 1981. In the old days the Arabs built their ships from wood, so he built his ship, the *Sohar*, from wood too. He sailed to China from Muscat, in Oman.

Was there really a King Mihraj, Sindbad's friend on his first voyage? There were great kings – Maharaja – in India at that time. Mihraj and Maharaja look nearly the same in some Arabic writing.

Was there a great King of Serendip? Yes. We know that Serendip was the old name for Sri Lanka. We also know that Arab and other merchants sailed to that island.

There were really voyages, but strange things happen in the Sindbad stories.

Are you ready? Let's sail with Sindbad!

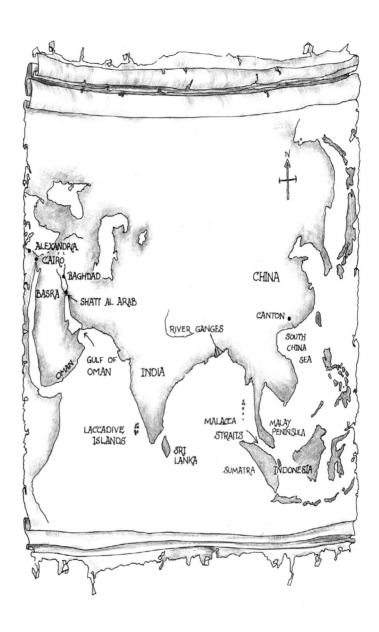

ALEXANDRIA
CAIRO
BAGHDAD
BASRA
SHATT AL ARAB
OMAN
GULF OF
OMAN
INDIA
LACCADIVE
ISLANDS
SRI
LANKA
RIVER GANGES
MALACCA
STRAITS
SUMATRA
CHINA
CANTON
SOUTH
CHINA
SEA
MALAY
PENINSULA
INDONESIA
N

The First Voyage

Sindbad the Sailor lived in Baghdad in the time of the great Khalif, Harun al-Rashid. Sindbad was a very rich man. He had a beautiful house in the best street in the city. The sun was very hot in the afternoons. Then he and his friends sat under the trees in the garden.

'I am rich now,' he told his friends. 'But after my father died, I made mistakes. So I went to sea. Listen! I will tell you about my first voyage. When I came back, I was a rich man. But on this voyage I was really afraid.'

◆

I was a young man then, and I was not careful with money. So my father's money went quickly.

I sold everything and, with the money, I bought the best goods. The next day, I took them to Basra. There, on the river, was an Arab ship, and I spoke to its captain. He answered me kindly.

'We are going to sail next week. There will be six merchants with their goods on the ship, and we will sail to the countries and islands of the east. There the merchants will sell their goods and buy other rich goods. They will sell them in their countries when they come back.'

'Can you take another merchant?' I asked. 'I want to sell some boxes of goods. I will give you a lot of money when I sell them.'

'Yes,' said the captain, 'I can take you.'

And so, the next week, we sailed down the great river, the Shatt al-Arab, and through the Gulf, and then to the east. We sailed for very many days and nights, and we stopped at cities and islands. There we sold and bought goods. One day we came to a very beautiful island, with trees and flowers and birds of many colours.

'I do not know this island,' the captain said. 'But it looks very beautiful. Perhaps we will find water there. I will take the ship near it.'

He brought the ship near the island. We went for a walk and looked for water.

I began to walk away from the ship. Some merchants found wood, and they made a fire on the island.

Suddenly, the island moved under my feet!

'Run, everybody!' the captain shouted. 'Run quickly to the ship! I made a dangerous mistake. This is not an island – it is a great fish. It was asleep on top of the water. But your fire woke it. Run for your lives!'

Everybody ran. But I had to run a long way and I could not get to the ship in time. The island-fish swam down – down – down under the sea, and I went down with it.

At the same time, a great wind came and took the ship away. When I got to the top of the water, I could not see the ship anywhere.

'I am going to die here in this great sea,' I cried. 'Nobody can help me now.'

But – Allah is good! – I found a box from the ship and I sat on it. Night came. The wind pushed me that night, and the next day and the next night.

In the morning, I was really afraid.

'This is my last day,' I thought. 'I am ill and nearly dead. My fingers are blue with cold. Tomorrow, I will fall into the sea and die.'

And then I saw it – an island! The wind took me to the island, and the sea threw me under a tree there. After that, I do not remember much. But I know that I could not move for two days.

'I have to find food and water now,' I thought. 'I do not want to die.'

So I tried to stand up ... but I could not. My feet hurt. I looked down at them.

Suddenly, the island moved under my feet!

'The fish tried to eat them,' I cried. 'I have to wash them in clean water.'

I started to look for food and water. It was difficult but I moved with my arms. Then I found a fruit tree near a little river and I stayed there for one or two days.

I ate the fruit from the tree and I drank the water from the little river. My feet were better and I felt stronger.

I had to move. I took some fruit with me, but I could not carry any water.

'There will be other rivers,' I thought.

But there was no drinking water, and there were no fruit trees. I saw no houses, no people – nothing.

I walked for three days, and I began to be afraid again.

'Am I the only person here?' I cried. 'Is this an island without people, animals or birds?'

Something moved a long way away. Was it a dangerous animal? Or was it a man? When I came near, I saw it. It was a beautiful horse, under a tree.

'This horse,' I thought, 'is the horse of a king or a very rich man.'

The animal saw me and made a loud noise. I jumped and I ran away. A man heard the noise and ran out from a cave.

'Nobody looks at the king's horse and lives!' he called angrily.

'Stop, do not kill me,' I said. 'I looked at the horse because it is so beautiful.'

'Who are you?' the man asked. 'And why are you here?'

'I am here,' I said, 'because Allah was good. My ship sailed to an island. I went for a walk under the trees, but the island moved under my feet!'

'How can an island move?' asked the man.

'It was not an island. It was a big fish,' I answered. 'And I fell into the sea. The captain and the other merchants got to the ship and they sailed away. I sat on a box for days. The wind brought me here.'

'Come to the cave,' said the man kindly. 'I can give you food and water. Allah was good to you. I come here only one week every month, with other men. We bring the king's best horses to this island. The food is good for them, but there is no food or water for men. Our city is a long way away. You cannot find your way there without help. But we are leaving tomorrow. Would you like to come with us?'

'Thank you,' I answered.

After a time, the other men came to the cave. Each man was with a beautiful horse. They heard my story and they were also very kind to me. The next day, I left with them on one of the king's beautiful horses.

On the way, they told me about their king.

'King Mihraj,' they said, 'is the greatest king in these islands. His people love him because he is kind to everybody. Merchants from every country come to our great city near the sea.'

When they arrived at the city, the men told King Mihraj about me. He sent for me and I told him my strange story.

'Allah was good to you!' he said. 'And we, too, will help you in every way.'

King Mihraj liked me, and he was very kind to me. One day, I went with his men to another island. They wanted to show me the strange fish there. One fish was bigger than a ship. And there was a fish with a bird's head.

'They are as strange as the island-fish,' I thought, 'but they are not as dangerous.'

I can speak to people from many countries. When the king heard this, he asked, 'Will you help the merchants and sailors in my city? A lot of people arrive here every day.'

'I will do that,' I answered.

After that, I saw the king every day. I told him about these merchants and their goods. I wrote everything in a book and showed the book to him.

I asked the captain of every ship about his voyage and about my city – Baghdad.

One day, a big ship came in from the east. The merchants began to sell their goods and buy goods in the city.

I spoke to the ship's captain.

'Are there other goods in the ship?' I asked.

'The merchants with me have no goods to sell now,' he said. 'But there are some boxes on the ship. A young merchant began the voyage with us, and the goods in the boxes were his. He is dead now. The sea took him. I am going to sell his goods here and take the money back to his people in the great city of Baghdad.'

Then I looked at the captain's face again. I knew him!

'What was his name?' I asked. 'What was the young merchant's name?'

'His name was Sindbad.'

I nearly fell to the ground.

'I am Sindbad,' I said. 'The goods are mine!'

The captain looked at me, half-angry and half-sad.

'What can I do?' he asked. 'You say that you are Sindbad. But perhaps you say that because you want his goods. The sea took Sindbad when the island moved. The sailors and the merchants on my ship saw it too.'

'Captain,' I said, 'listen to my story. Then you will know that I am Sindbad.'

And I told him my story from the time of our first meeting in Basra.

'And do you remember the fish-island?' I asked. 'Your merchants made a fire there and it moved. I fell into the sea, but I sat on a box from the ship for days.'

He stopped me and began to smile.

'It *is* you, Sindbad!' he said.

The other merchants came and talked to me.

'Allah is good,' they said, 'and we are also very happy.'

Then the captain gave me my goods. I sold them and with the money I bought other beautiful goods. I sent them to King Mihraj.

'Thank you,' he said, 'but I do not understand. You came here with nothing, and now you are giving me these beautiful things. How can you do this?'

'My ship is now in your city,' I told him. 'It came in yesterday. My goods and boxes were on the ship.'

King Mihraj said thank you to Allah for me, and he also gave me many beautiful things.

The ship was ready the next day. I said goodbye to the king.

'I am sad,' I told him. 'I do not want to leave your beautiful country and its great and good king. But I have to see my dear city of Baghdad again.'

'Yes, Sindbad,' he said. 'You have to go home now. I will be sad without you. But thank you for your help.'

After a very long voyage, the ship arrived in Basra. From there, I made the journey to Baghdad. My friends were very happy when they saw me. I bought a beautiful house and lived there, rich and happy, for some years.

Tomorrow, I will tell you about my second voyage.

The Second Voyage

I was happy for some time in Baghdad. I had my beautiful house, friends and money.

But I began to feel bored. I wanted to see other countries and cities again. I wanted to buy and sell in these places. I bought the best goods in Baghdad, and I sailed, with other merchants, on a beautiful, new ship.

We sailed from place to place, and from island to island. We always went to the south and east.

After a long time, we came to a beautiful island. It had green trees and fruit and flowers and rivers of good, clean water. But there were no people anywhere. Some sailors looked for clean water, and some merchants wanted to walk on the island.

'I will come with you,' I said.

The flowers were really beautiful. I walked through the trees and found some very big, beautiful flowers. I sat down near them. There was a warm wind and I fell asleep. When I woke up, I was suddenly afraid. There was nobody there – no sailors, no merchants, no people.

'I am very stupid!' I cried. 'I am here again, a long way from Baghdad, on an island without people!'

I climbed to the top of a tree and I looked out to sea. My ship was out there. It looked very small. Then I looked down. I saw only trees – and more trees.

I looked again. There was something a long way away, big and white and round. Was it the top of a house?

I walked for many hours and arrived there in the evening.

'It is not a house,' I thought. 'There is no door. What is it? Is it a giant egg?'

I thought for a long time. Then something moved across the light of the sun.

'Why is the sky dark?' I cried.

I looked up. Above my head was a giant bird. I remembered the sailors' stories about giant birds.

'There is one very big bird,' they said. 'That bird gives elephants to its babies for food.'

'So this,' I thought, 'is an egg from that bird. Now the mother is going to sit on it.'

I was right. The giant bird sat on the egg and fell asleep there. I had a good idea.

'When it wants to eat, it will fly away,' I thought. 'Perhaps it will go to a better place, a place with people in it. The bird can take me with it.'

I put some clothes round my arms and legs, then round the bird's leg. I worked very slowly.

'I cannot wake the bird,' I thought, 'or it will hurt me.'

In the morning, the giant bird woke up and flew away ... up high into the sky. It could not see me, and it took me a long, long way, over seas and islands and mountains and valleys. Then it came down in a valley with great walls of mountains round it.

My dangerous journey was not at an end. The giant bird came down on a big snake. I was really afraid then. I pulled my clothes from the bird's leg and ran behind a great stone.

When the bird flew away with the snake, I came out. I looked round me. There were other big snakes in the valley. Some were as long as a ship. I watched them when they went into great holes under the ground.

'They sleep in those holes under the ground in the day,' I thought, 'and come out for their food at night. So in the daytime I can look for a way out of the valley.'

I could not climb out of that valley. But I saw diamonds on the valley floor. They shone in the sunlight. They were very good diamonds – big and beautiful.

'But I do not want diamonds,' I thought. 'I want to get out of this valley.'

Night came and great snakes began to come out of the ground. I was near a small cave, so I ran inside. I found a big stone and moved it into the mouth of the cave. All night I listened to the noise of the snakes – Ssssssss! – but they could not get to me.

In the morning, I came out of the cave.

'I have to find a way out of the valley,' I thought. 'I do not want the snakes to kill me.'

I began to look again. Suddenly, there was a loud noise, and a dead animal fell to the ground near me. And there were diamonds on it! Then I remembered the stories about the Valley of Diamonds.

Merchants cannot get the diamonds from the valley because it is too dangerous. So they kill animals and throw them down. The meat falls on the diamonds. Some diamonds – but not the biggest ones – stay on the animal. Then great birds come down into the valley. They take the meat and fly up with it to their babies on the mountains. The merchants make a loud noise and the birds fly away. Then the merchants take the diamonds from the meat.

'A bird brought me here,' I thought, 'so a bird can take me away.'

I opened my food-bag and put the biggest and best diamonds in it. I put some of my clothes round my arms and legs, then round the animal meat. I waited there on my back, with the meat on top of me.

After a time, one of the great birds flew down and took the meat. It flew up out of the valley with it – and with me. I was very high in the sky. I closed my eyes because I was afraid.

At the top of a mountain above the valley, the baby birds waited. But the merchants waited too. When the bird came to the mountain top, they made a loud noise. The bird flew away and the meat fell to the ground. Then the merchants came for the diamonds. I stood up – red from the meat.

The merchants were afraid when they saw me.

'Why is this animal not dead?' they asked.

'Do not be afraid,' I said, 'I am a man too. You saw the bird? It brought your meat up from the Valley of the Diamonds, but it brought me with it. There are no diamonds on the meat, but I have some. They are the biggest and best diamonds. I will happily give you some.'

I stood up – red from the meat.

'Thank you,' they said kindly. 'Now come with us, and we will find you bread and water.'

I sat down with them. We ate and drank.

'Nobody comes back from that dangerous valley,' they told me. 'You are the first person.'

'Allah helped me,' I said. Then I slept for hours.

The next day, I went with the merchants. We walked and climbed over mountains. Then, after some weeks, we came to the sea.

After a short voyage in a boat, we arrived at an island. I saw many strange animals there. One animal, I remember, was tall and thin with a tusk on its head. This animal killed a smaller animal. A giant bird flew down. It took away the dead animal and flew up to the mountain top with it.

'I am happier on the ground with you, my kind friends,' I said to the merchants.

'We are happy too,' they answered. 'Now we will leave this island with its strange animals and sail to other islands. There we will sell our diamonds.'

'Where will we go?' I asked the merchants.

'From island to island,' they answered. 'We know many people here and they buy our diamonds. We have better and bigger diamonds because you gave them to us, Sindbad. So we will help you. You can sell your diamonds too.'

'Thank you,' I answered.

◆

We sailed. I sold many diamonds on those islands and the people were kind to me. I made money and with it I bought goods. I sold these goods on other islands. One day, I shouted happily to the merchants, 'Now I have money and I can sail back to my city! Will you help me to find a ship for Baghdad?'

'Yes, Sindbad,' they answered, 'but we will be sorry. We do not want to say goodbye to you.'

So I came home to Baghdad, a very rich man, with the biggest of my diamonds and other goods.

'Now I will stay at home here,' I said, 'in my beautiful house, with my money. I will be happy with my friends, and I will never go to sea again.'

I arrived at my house, and I gave my friends and family diamonds and other rich things from the countries and islands of my voyage. Then I went into the city and gave money to people without anything.

After two or three weeks, I forgot about the giant bird, the giant snakes and the Valley of Diamonds, and the other strange things on my voyage.

I bought fine clothes and good food. My house was open for everybody and many people came. They wanted to hear about my voyage. I talked to them and I began to be bored with my happy life in Baghdad.

So I went to sea again!

Tomorrow, I will tell you about my third voyage.

The Third Voyage

I sailed from Basra with other merchants in a very good ship. We went from country to country and from island to island, and we sold everything.

Then one day a strong wind began to take us a long way away.

'Where are we going?' we cried. 'We do not want to go with this wind.'

For four days the angry wind pushed us, and then we came to an island. The captain was really afraid.

'We cannot sail away into this wind,' he said. 'But I know about this island. It is the Island of Zughb. Its people are small and ugly. They have yellow eyes and dark brown hair. Thousands of people come on to ships. Please, please do not fight them. They will get angry and kill you.'

He stopped for a minute, then cried, 'They are here!'

The monkey-men came from the island. They were very ugly. There were thousands, and we could not stop them. They ran and jumped round the ship. They put the sailors and merchants on the island, and they sailed our ship away.

We started to look for food and water and we found a fruit tree next to a small river. But we were very afraid of the monkey-men when we sat down.

'There are more monkey-men on the island,' we thought. 'They will kill us. What can we do? Where can we go?'

'We have to stay away from those dangerous men,' said one sailor. 'I will climb that tree and look for a place.'

From the top of the tree, he saw a big stone house.

'We can go there, away from the monkey-men,' he shouted.

'Let's go now!' we called. 'We can take the fruit and water with us. It is too dangerous here.'

We ran to the house. It was very tall with a great door.

'Look!' said my friends. 'The door is open. We can go in and sleep. There are no monkey-men here.'

We went into the house. It had one very big room and we fell asleep there. The sound of heavy feet woke us up.

'What is that?' we cried. 'Are there thousands of monkey-men? Are they going to kill us?'

The door of the room began to open. We sat up and waited. We were very afraid.

It was a giant! He was very, very big. He was a man, but he was as tall as the tallest tree. His eyes were as red as fire. His mouth was as wide as a cave and his teeth were as long as elephant tusks.

We watched him with our mouths open. The giant came in and closed the door behind him. He took wood from a box and he made a big fire with it in the room.

Then he looked at us. He saw my rich clothes and took me up in his hands. But I was not a fat man. Under all those clothes, I was really not fatter than his finger. So he threw me down and took up another man. In the end the giant found the fattest man.

The giant cooked that man over his fire. Then he ate him! After that, he sat down near the fire and slept.

The next day, the giant left the room. But he shut the door, so we could not get out.

We were afraid and cried loudly, 'What can we do? He will come back when he is hungry. Who will he eat next?'

We were right. In the evening, the giant came back. He found a strong man – the ship's captain – and he cooked him! And ate him! And slept.

In the morning, the giant went out and shut the door again.

'We have to do something,' I said. 'We cannot kill him – he is too big. But I have an idea . . .'

The other men listened to me.

That evening, the giant came into the room. He took a man and cooked him. He ate the man, and fell asleep.

Then we began to work quickly. Two men put wood into the fire and made it red-hot. Two other men took wood from the fire and made a hole in the great door. Other men took wood from the giant's box. We carried that with us.

Everything was ready. I called: 'Now!'

We pushed the red-hot wood into the giant's eyes, and then we ran past him. We climbed through the hole in the door. It was difficult because we carried with us the wood for our boats.

But we ran as quickly as we could. The giant's shouts hurt our ears! When we came to the sea, we built our boats. Then we sailed away. We heard a loud shout and we turned our heads. There were *three* giants!

In the end the giant found the fattest man.

When the three giants saw us in the boats, they threw great stones at us. Each stone was as big as a house. Some stones fell into the sea, but some hit our boats. The men in those boats died.

The stones did not hit my boat. We took it out to sea. But then a strong wind came. It pushed us day after day, through angry seas, before it threw us onto an island.

There were three people in my boat. We were very hungry and thirsty, but we were not dead. We found fruit trees and a small river. There we ate and drank. We said thank you to Allah. Then we fell asleep on the ground; we were tired after that dangerous voyage across the sea.

A loud noise woke us up – Sssssss!

A giant snake started to move over the ground and it took one of my friends into its mouth. He went down – down – down inside. For a time we could hear him. Then the noise stopped. He was dead.

The snake stayed there all night. We did not move or speak. But in the end it went away, and we said, 'What can we do? It will come back tonight, and it will eat another man. We ran away from the giant because he wanted to eat us. But now the snake wants to eat us too.'

We ate fruit and drank water. And we thought hard.

'We will look for a cave,' I said to my friend. 'The snake cannot find us there.'

But we could not find a cave.

'It is nearly night,' I said. 'The snake will look for us then. Let's climb a tree and sleep there.'

We went up the tallest tree. I was stronger than my friend, and I could go higher in the tree.

Night came and the great snake was there again. It found our tree and came up it. It caught my friend with its mouth, and I heard his last shout from inside the snake. I sat in the tree. I could not move because I was too afraid.

In the morning, the snake was not there.

'What shall I do?' I thought. 'It will come back tonight and kill me. Shall I jump into the sea? Is that better?'

I ate some fruit from the trees, and I thought ... and I thought. I remembered Allah.

'Thank you!' I cried to him. 'There are no monkey-men here!'

Then, on the sea, I saw wood from the boats and it gave me an idea. I worked very hard. I made a box from the wood and I sat inside it. Then I waited for the snake.

Night came, and I heard the snake outside the box. Its big mouth came near my head ... near my arms ... near my feet ... near my legs. The box was small and I could not move inside it. The snake tried again and again, but it could not eat me. The wood was too strong.

It moved away.

'Thank you again, Allah!' I cried. 'I am not dead!'

In the morning, I made a boat from the wood. I put fruit and water in it, and then I took it out to sea, away from that dangerous island.

I do not want to remember the days on that open boat. I was red under the hot sun and the sea was angry again. But in the end I saw a ship, and the sailors saw me. They came and took me into their ship. They were very kind to me.

'Where are you from?' they asked me.

'From Basra,' I said. 'And I want to go back to my city, Baghdad. I want to see my family and friends again.'

'But why are you here?' they asked. 'You are a long way from home.'

I told the captain and other merchants on the ship about the monkey-men, and the giant and the snake.

'I am not dead because Allah helped me,' I said.

'We will take you to Basra,' the captain said, 'but we have to visit some other places first. The merchants want to sell and buy goods. Then we will wait for a good wind and sail back to Basra.'

At the next stop, the sailors carried up the merchants' goods.

'Bring up Sindbad's goods,' the captain said to his men. 'We will sell them here and take the money to his people in Baghdad.'

'Sindbad's goods?' I asked. 'Do they have these letters on them?'

I wrote some letters. Those letters were always on my goods and boxes.

'Yes,' he said. 'But how do you know that? They are the goods of a dead merchant. He died on an island.'

'He is not dead,' I said. 'I am Sindbad. I fell asleep on the island and a bird took me to the Valley of Diamonds. Giant snakes tried to kill me, but a bird took me to the mountain top. And merchants found me there.'

'It is difficult for me,' said the captain. 'What can I do? Perhaps you are not Sindbad but you want to take his goods.'

'I am a good man,' I said. 'I do not want to take another man's goods.'

The captain said nothing.

Many merchants were on the ship and they heard my story. One man came and spoke to the captain.

'I know this man,' he said, 'because I was on the Diamond Mountain at that time. I remember it well. The bird flew up to the mountain top with meat and Sindbad. We were afraid. Was he a man or an animal? But he had with him the best and biggest diamonds from the valley. He was kind and he gave me some. I left the mountain after that and he went with other merchants.'

The captain listened to him and thought about his words. Then he smiled at me and his men brought up my goods from the ship. I sold them and bought other goods. We sailed to Basra.

After my third voyage I was a very, very rich man. I gave money to my family and friends and to other people.

'I want to live happily in Baghdad now,' I told them. 'There will never be a fourth voyage for me.'

But there was a fourth voyage, and tomorrow I will tell you about it.

The Fourth Voyage

One day some merchants came to my house. When we spoke about our voyages to strange countries and islands, we remembered only the good times. We forgot about the other, bad times.

'Let's sail to the east again,' we said. 'It will be interesting for us and it will make us rich.'

We sailed south and east to rich countries. We sailed from island to island, from sea to sea, from country to country. In each place we sold and bought goods.

We were a long way from home when one night a big wind pushed our ship over. Great seas, as high as mountains, hit it and threw us into the water.

'This is my last hour,' I thought.

But some wood from the ship came past me, and I put my arms round it. I helped other merchants and sailors to catch the wood too. The next day, the sea threw us onto an island. We were half-dead.

We stayed in the same place that night because we could not move. We were too tired and weak. So in the morning, some men found us there. I call them men, but they were closer to animals – very ugly animals.

They took us to their king. He spoke to them, and they brought food for us. It was strange food, but the other merchants and the sailors ate some. I could not eat it. I felt ill when I looked at it.

Something sad happened. That food changed my friends. They began to eat very quickly and with two hands. Then I remembered the stories about these animal-men. When they catch people from another country, they give them this food. Then people only want to eat. They eat and eat. The king and his animal-men like to eat these fat men.

'Stop!' I cried to the men from our ship. But I could not help them. They could only think about the food.

Day after day my friends ate. The animal-men stayed near them and gave them more food. I was ill and thin because I could not eat anything. But the animal-men were not angry with me because they had other fat people for food.

'I cannot help my friends,' I thought, 'but I can leave this dangerous place. I do not want to die here.'

My friends never left the animal-men, but nobody watched me, the thin man. So one day I moved away into the trees and nobody saw me.

After a time I found some fruit. I knew that fruit and I was not afraid of it. The food made me stronger, and I walked quickly. For days I ate fruit and walked.

Then I saw some men. They were afraid of me, and they tried to kill me. But I called to them, 'In the name of Allah, hear me!'

I told them my name and about my city – Baghdad. And they said, 'We come every year from our country to this island, but we are always afraid of the animal-men. We know that they eat men. Nobody gets away from them. Come with us.'

When they went back to their island, my new friends took me with them. Their king heard about me. He was very kind and gave me a room in his great house. He asked me about my voyages and the great city of Baghdad.

His city was rich in many ways. But one thing was strange. The king and his people went everywhere on horses. They were very good horses, but they had no saddles. One day I asked the king, 'Why, great King, do you not have a saddle for your horse?'

'A saddle?' he said. 'What is that?'

'Can I make a saddle for you?' I asked. 'Then you will know. A saddle is a great help to a man on a horse.'

I made a very good saddle for the king and I put it on his horse. He tried it and he was very happy with it. After that, every great man in the country wanted a saddle. I was very rich again, and I was happy. I was a friend of the king and of the great men of the country.

One day the king spoke to me. 'You are a brother to us now,' he said. 'But you can be more than that.'

'Tell me,' I said. 'I will always listen to you.'

'I want you to marry. There is a rich and very beautiful woman in this city, the daughter of a friend. Would you like to marry her?'

'Yes,' I told him. 'I am a rich man. I would like a wife.'

So I married. My wife *was* rich and beautiful. But I also loved her, and she loved me. And so I was happy.

One day, the wife of a friend died. I went to my friend because I wanted to help him at this sad time. But he was not only sad – he was really ill.

'Allah will be unhappy when he sees you,' I told him. 'You have to get better. You *can* learn to live without her.'

'What?' he cried. 'In this country a man has to follow his dead wife. This afternoon they will throw my dead wife into the Cave of the Dead, and they will send me down there too. I will die with her.'

'That is a very bad idea!' I said.

That afternoon, people took his dead wife outside the city. They moved a great stone from a hole in the mountain and threw her down into the Cave of the Dead. Then they put my friend down into the cave after her. They put the great stone back, and men stayed outside.

'Nobody can go near the cave,' I thought. 'I cannot call to my friend or help him in any way.'

I spoke to the king about it.

'I cannot change the ways of my country,' he said.

And then my dear wife was very ill and died! People came and took her to the Cave of the Dead.

My wife was rich and beautiful. But I also loved her . . .

'You cannot take me with her,' I said. 'I am not from this country, so it is different for me.'

'You are from here now,' they said.

And they took me to the hole in the mountain and pulled away the great stone. I went down into the cave, with bread and water for seven days. Men pushed the stone in place and I could see nothing.

'Help me, Allah!' I cried.

There was a little light in the cave. They always put dead people into the cave with their diamonds, so there were beautiful diamonds everywhere. They shone in the light.

I saw a small animal. I tried to catch it, but it ran away.

'Animals will know a way in and out of this cave,' I thought. 'They can take me to it.'

I tried to catch an animal. And I tried again. And again. A thousand times.

In the end I caught one. The animal pulled me after it to one end of the cave, a very long way from the great stone. It went through a hole between some stones and ran outside. I could see blue sky! But I was too big. I could not follow it. I pulled away the small stones, day after day. Then I was outside!

I was near the sea, at the foot of a small mountain. I knew about the place, but nobody from the city could climb down there. It was too dangerous.

'I have to find food and water now,' I thought.

I walked to a little river, and there was a fruit tree near it. I drank and ate. Then I sat down and thought.

'I will wait for a ship,' I thought. 'I want a ship to take me away from this country. But first I want to go back into the Cave of the Dead for some diamonds. Will I find the way out again? It is a long way, and very dark.'

I thought about this for a long time.

'I have to go back. I can sell the diamonds for the voyage to Basra. I will go now before I am too afraid.'

It was not too difficult. I went into the cave again and again and brought out thousands of diamonds. I put them in bags from the clothes of the dead people.

And then I waited for a ship.

When a ship came for water from the river, I told my story to the captain. I did not tell him everything, because I did not want people from my new country to hear about me. I did not want to go back to the cave.

I wanted to give some of the diamonds to the captain, but he said, 'We are men of Basra. When somebody wants our help, we take him into our ship. We give him food and drink and clothes. Then we help him on his way to his country. We never take money or other things from him, because we help him for the love of Allah.'

In time, the ship's voyage ended at Basra, and I went from there to Baghdad.

My friends were happy, and I gave money and food and clothes to people in my city.

And I said, 'Never again! That was my last voyage!'

It was *not* my last voyage. I will tell you about it tomorrow.

The Fifth Voyage

When I thought about my voyages later, I remembered only the good things, not the bad things.

One day I saw a beautiful new ship. I bought the ship and sailed, with other merchants, on my fifth voyage.

We sailed from city to city, and from island to island, and from sea to sea. We sold and bought goods. And we saw many new places.

One day we came to a big island. There were no people, no trees, no rivers – nothing. Some merchants went for a walk on the island, but I stayed on the ship. My friends found something very big and white on the ground.

I was afraid and shouted to them from the ship, 'Come away! Quickly! It is a giant bird's egg.'

But the merchants took big stones and broke the egg. Inside they found a young bird. It began to cry and a loud noise answered from high in the sky.

'Run!' I shouted again. 'That is the noise of the parent birds. They know the baby bird is afraid. They are coming to help it. They will kill you.'

But the merchants took the young bird from the egg and ate it.

'You are stupid men!' I shouted. 'Now the parent birds will kill us!'

The two great birds – the father and the mother – flew over us and the sky went dark.

'Now we are dead men,' I cried.

But then the birds flew away again.

'Quickly!' I called to the merchants. 'We will sail now. Run!'

The merchants ran to the ship, and the captain and his men took us quickly out to sea.

'The captain is a clever man,' I thought. 'Perhaps we can get away from those angry birds.'

I was wrong! We saw the great birds above us. Each bird carried a stone and the stone was as big as a house. The first bird flew over us, and the stone fell. The captain sailed the ship quickly and the stone fell into the sea. But the stone was heavy and the sea flew up in mountains of water.

The captain could not sail us away from the next stone. It fell on us, and that was the end of my beautiful ship. The stone killed many merchants and sailors.

I fell into the sea and found some wood from my ship. The wind and the sea took me, after four days and nights, to an island.

But the merchants took big stones and broke the egg.

I saw a river of clean water and trees with fruit and cried, 'Thank you, Allah!'

I ate and drank. Then I began to look for people. I walked all night.

Early the next morning, I met an old man near the river. His hair was grey and he looked ill.

'He is an old sailor,' I thought. 'Perhaps the sea brought him to this island. He can help me, and I can help him.'

I went to the old man.

'Can I help you?' I asked. 'The angry wind brought me here. Are there other people here?'

He looked at me and said nothing.

'Can I help you?' I asked again.

Again he said nothing, but he looked at the little river, then at me.

'He wants me to carry him across the river,' I thought.

I wanted to help this man because he was old and tired. I put him on my back to go across the water. Then he quickly put his legs round me. His legs were very strong. I tried to push him away, but he kicked me. Then he took me in his hands and legs and feet, and I nearly died. I closed my eyes.

Later, when I opened my eyes, the old man kicked me again. He pushed me and kicked me day after day. At night I could sleep on the ground, but his legs were always round me. In the daytime I could only eat fruit and drink water with him. He was always there, but he never spoke.

'I want to die!' I cried every day. 'I cannot live with this! How am I going to get away from this old man? I will never see my city again!'

After many weeks of this sad life, I found a fruit. When it is old, this fruit makes a very strong drink. I drank, and I felt warm and happy. I cried, 'This is good wine! Very good! Ah! Now I feel stronger!'

The old man kicked me. He was angry because I liked the drink. He wanted to try it too. I gave it to him and he drank. He

28

liked it, and he drank – and drank again. When he drank, his legs fell away from me. I quickly threw him to the ground. He could not get up again.

I hit him on the head with a big stone. Then I ran away.

After that, I went down to the sea. There was a ship there. The sailors came to me and asked, 'Who are you? Why are you here?'

'The wind and sea brought me to this island,' I told them. 'But that was better than my life here.'

'Why do you say that?' they asked. 'There is good fruit and water on this island.'

'I met an old man,' I answered. 'He sat on me and I had to carry him. He pushed and kicked me every day. I am nearly dead. I ran away from him today.'

They looked at me strangely. 'Allah was good to you!' they cried. 'That was the Sheikh al-Bahr, the Old Man of the Sea. No man gets away from the old man's legs. He kills many good sailors. We always come on to this island in large numbers, because we are afraid of him.'

'Why do you come here?' I asked.

'We come for coconuts,' they said. 'We sell them and make money. Come, and we will show you. Take these big bags for the coconuts and this small bag of stones.'

I carried the bag of stones in one hand, and the big bags in the other hand, and I walked to a place near the sea. There were many tall coconut trees. I looked at them.

'I cannot climb these trees,' I said. 'There are no places for my feet. How can I get coconuts?'

The men began to laugh.

'There are monkeys up there in the trees,' they told me. 'Throw the stones at them. They will get angry and they will throw coconuts at you.'

I did this. It was easy! I worked every day with the other men. I worked hard because I wanted money for a ship back to Basra.

We cut away the outside of the coconuts and put the fruit into our big bags. Then we went back to the men's ship and sailed to Comorin and the islands near it. They paid us well for the coconuts, and we bought wood and other things.

We sailed again. After many days and nights, we arrived in Basra and I left for my city, Baghdad. I was a richer man when I came back to my country. I gave away some money, and said; 'Never again! There will be no voyages now.'

But there was another voyage, and I will tell you about it tomorrow.

The Sixth Voyage

I wanted to see India. So I took goods and men and sold and bought goods in its great cities. I saw the countries and the people. I went by road – the sea was too dangerous!

But I came to the end of the road near the mouth of the great river Ganges. There I found a ship. It was ready for a voyage to the south and east.

'I will make one last voyage,' I thought.

It was a long voyage, and it was dangerous. The wind took us out of our way, and then the sea pushed us very quickly. The captain looked at a mountain in front of us.

'We are dead men!' he shouted. 'This is the end! Can you see that mountain? There is a cave at its foot. The sea will take our ship into it. I cannot stop it now. There is no way out from the cave. When a man goes in there, he dies!'

The sailors tried to sail the ship out of the fast water, but – no – they could do nothing. The water moved quickly into that great cave. The mountain came nearer and nearer to us.

Suddenly the water carried our ship into the cave. And then, inside, the ship hit stone walls and broke. There were men and wood everywhere in the water.

'Help us! Help!' they cried.

Suddenly the water carried our ship into the cave.

I tried but I could do nothing. The water was too fast. Everything went black.

'I am dead,' I thought.

But I was not dead.

'Where are you, my friends?' I called.

I listened. Nobody shouted, but I could hear the water. There was a strong wind and it pushed me through the cave – not in the water, but on some wood.

There was no day and no night, but my journey through those black caves was very long. I was tired and afraid. I fell asleep.

After a long time, I woke up and thought, 'This water comes into the mountain from the sea. So that water has to leave the mountain at the other end. I will come out with the water. Perhaps there will be men there.'

I moved with the water for a long time and I fell asleep again. I woke to the sound of shouts. I opened my eyes and looked round me.

I was on my back, on the wood from the ship, next to a great river. People looked down at me. The noise came from them.

'Where am I?' I asked.

They said nothing.

'Who are you?' I asked. 'Can you help me?'

They answered me then, but I could not understand them because they spoke no Arabic. One man knew a little Arabic and he spoke to me kindly.

'You are in the country of the great king of Serendip.'

I was happy then because I knew about this great king and his country.

'We are cutting a way from this great river to our homes,' the Arabic-speaker said. 'We want water there. We know this river comes from those mountains. We also know that no man can walk here from those mountains because it is too dangerous. So how are you here?'

'Please,' I said. 'Can you give me bread and water? I am very hungry and thirsty. Then I will tell you my story.'

The people brought me food and drink. I told them about the cave near the sea.

'The sea went into that cave,' I said. 'And our ship went with it. It broke on the stone walls.'

I began to cry.

'My friends are dead! I was very afraid on that long and dangerous journey in the dark!'

The Arabic-speaker told my story to the other men. They shouted to him.

'They say,' the man told me, 'that you have to tell this story to the king. We will take you to him now.'

They brought a horse for me and we left the river. After a journey of three days, we arrived at the king's city and the men went to see him.

The king heard my story. He gave me rooms and the best clothes and food and other good things. He sent for me day after day, and I told him the story of my six voyages. He asked questions about Baghdad.

'I know of your city,' the king said, 'and of your great Khalif, Harun al-Rashid. He is a good man.'

One day, I heard about a ship on its way to Basra.

'Go,' said the king. 'And please talk to your Khalif about me. I shall give you a letter for him, and many rich things for you and him.'

'Thank you,' I answered. 'I will happily take them for you.'

The letter began:

From the King of Serendip, King of the Indies, to his friend, the great Khalif Harun al-Rashid.

And he sent many beautiful things from Serendip.

I had a good voyage to Basra, and I took everything to the Khalif. He heard my story and spoke kindly to me.

Then I went back to my house and met my friends again. I gave away money to people without anything.

The Seventh Voyage

'I will make no other journeys, and no other voyages,' I told my friends in Baghdad. 'I am not young now. I am going to stay at home and be happy in my house and gardens.'

One day I was with my friends when the Khalif Harun al-Rashid sent for me.

'I want you,' the great Khalif said, 'to take my answer to the King of Serendip.'

'I will go now,' I said.

The Khalif's men found me the best ship and made it ready for sea. We sailed when the wind could take us to the east. We carried the Khalif's letter and the richest and most beautiful things from Baghdad, Alexandria, Cairo and the cities of the west.

'I am very happy you are here again, Sindbad!' said the king. 'And thank you for the letter from your great Khalif. When you go back to Baghdad, you will take beautiful things with you.'

'Thank you,' I answered.

We began the voyage home. After three days at sea, we saw a pirate ship near us. There were hundreds of pirates in five or six boats, and they quickly took our ship. They sailed with us to an island, and there they sold us.

A merchant bought me, a good and kind man.

'Can you kill animals with a gun?' he asked me.

'Yes.'

'Good. In this country, when we buy a man from the pirates, he kills elephants for us. We sell the tusks and give money to the pirates. I will take you to the elephants tonight, and you can begin.'

When we came to that place, I had to climb a tree.

'Wait there for the elephants, and then kill one. I will come in the morning. I will take you and the elephant's tusks to the city.'

I waited a long time, but then an elephant came near my tree. I killed it with my gun. The merchant came in the morning, and he was happy with me and the dead elephant.

'You work well,' he said. 'But remember one thing when you try to kill elephants.'

'What is that?' I asked.

'You have to kill it the first time, or it will kill you.'

'I understand,' I said. 'I do not want to die here, a long way away from my home.'

That afternoon, I met two other men in the trees. They were from other ships. They also had to kill elephants and make money for the pirates.

'We will not have a long life,' they told me. 'It is a dangerous job. Other elephants will come and kill us.'

I thought about their words.

'I will not climb the same tree every time,' I thought. 'I will not try to kill an elephant when I see other elephants near me. And I *have* to kill the elephant the first time or it will run away. Then it will bring other elephants to me.'

For a long time, I killed an elephant every night, and I always killed them the first time. The merchant was happy.

'You work better than the other men,' he said. 'From today you will have one tusk out of every ten. When you have a hundred tusks, you can take them home to your country.'

I worked hard night after night because I wanted to see my family and friends. I had nearly a hundred tusks! Then, one night, an elephant got away and I could not kill it.

I was afraid. 'Will this elephant come back and kill me?' I cried.

I waited for the night, high up in my tree. Then I heard a loud noise. I looked down at the ground and saw elephants – hundreds of them! – at the foot of my tree.

'I am going to die here!' I cried. 'Nobody can help me! What can I do?'

I climbed higher in the tree but the elephants came nearer. They stood at the bottom of the tree and waited.

'What are they thinking?' I asked.

I saw the answer to my question. The elephants began to pull the tree out of the ground. The tree moved under me.

I closed my eyes and waited to die. But the elephants took me from the tree and put me on the back of the biggest elephant. Then they left the tree on the ground and began to walk slowly away. We went through valley after valley.

We came to a small valley in the mountains, and there they stopped. I was afraid again. Why was I here with these elephants? Why was I not dead?

Then I looked round me. There were hundreds . . . thousands of dead elephants. Elephants came and died here! The other elephants stood next to me and looked at me. They did not try to hurt me. I began to understand. They wanted to tell me something with their eyes.

I thought; 'They are asking me "Why do you kill us for our tusks? Look here! Look at these tusks! We do not want them. Take them and tell the men from the city. They have to stop killing us."'

'I understand you now!' I shouted to them. 'Take me back to the city. I will tell the other men.'

The elephants stood and looked at me.

'Will you take me back?' I asked them again. 'I can tell the other men about the tusks here and they will not kill you. Please take me back and I can help you.'

The elephants understood me. They began to turn round slowly and walk away from that place.

I looked at the dead elephants on the ground for the last time and I felt sad.

We went back to the city and I found my merchant.

'You have to come with me,' I told him.

There were hundreds … thousands of dead elephants.

'Why?' he asked.

'There is a place with hundreds and thousands of tusks on dead elephants. The elephants took me there last night. They say we can take them. We can sell them.'

He laughed.

'But elephants cannot talk!' he said. 'Can we really take them? How do you know?'

'They told me with their eyes,' I said. 'I spoke to them and they understood me.'

We found the place again and the merchant was very happy with me. He looked, and looked again.

'The merchants in the city can sell these tusks for a hundred years!' he said. 'We do not have to kill elephants now. I am going back to the city and I will tell people.'

'Thank you,' I said.

From that day, they stopped killing elephants!

They gave me tusks and I sold them. With the money, I found a ship for Basra.

So I sailed home.

That was my last voyage! Allah was good to me then!

ACTIVITIES

The First Voyage

Before you read

1 This book is about Sindbad's journeys by sea. Sindbad lives in Baghdad. Discuss these questions.
   a Where is Baghdad? Can you find it on the map on page vi?
   b There are other cities on the map. Which countries are they in?
2 Look at the Word List at the back of the book. Find words for:
   a animals. b people. c places.
3 Look at the picture on page 3 and answer these questions.
   a What can you see?
   b What do you think is going to happen to:
   the men? the ship?

While you read

4 What happens first? What happens next? Number these sentences, 1–9.
   a Sindbad finds a box from the ship.   .....
   b Sindbad and the captain meet again.   .....
   c Sindbad goes to Basra.   .....
   d Sindbad goes down under the sea.   .....
   e Sindbad buys a beautiful house in Baghdad.   .....
   f The ship stops at a beautiful island.   .....
   g The ship sails through the Gulf to the East.   .....
   h Sindbad meets King Mihraj.   .....
   i Sindbad walks for three days.   .....

After you read

5 Answer these questions.
   a Why does Sindbad go on his first voyage?
   b Why does he lose his goods?
   c How does he get his goods back again?
   d What does he do when he arrives back in Baghdad?
6 Talk to another student. What do you know about King Mihraj?

The Second Voyage

Before you read

7 Discuss these questions: Do you think Sindbad will be happy now in Baghdad? Why (not)?

8 Work with another student. Have this conversation.

Student A: You are Sindbad. You are in Baghdad. You want to go on another voyage. Tell your friend why.

Student B: You are Sindbad's friend. Why does Sindbad want to leave? Ask him. Why do you want him to stay? Tell him.

While you read

9 Finish each sentence. Find the second half below.

a We sailed from place to place,

b When I woke up,

c There was something a long way away,

d The giant bird sat on the egg

e I put some clothes round my arms and legs,

f I pulled my clothes from the bird's legs,

g They were very good diamonds –

h I waited there on my back,

i After a time, one of the great birds flew down,

j I made money

then round the bird's leg.

big and beautiful.

and ran behind a great stone.

and took the meat.

with the meat on top of me.

and from island to island.

and fell asleep there.

big and white and round.

I was suddenly afraid.

and with it I bought goods.

After you read

10 Discuss these questions.

a How do the merchants usually get diamonds from the Valley of the Diamonds?

b How does Sindbad take diamonds from there?

The Third Voyage

Before you read

11 In the next story Sindbad meets a giant and then a big snake. What will happen? Think of a story with another student.

12 Look at the picture on page 16. Who do you think the men are? Why are they crying?

While you read.

13 Who or what:

    a has yellow eyes and dark brown hair?   ....

    b sails the ship away?   ....

    c is very tall and has red eyes?   ....

    d eats some of the men?   ....

    e throws stones at the boats?   ....

    f also eats people?   ....

    g tries to eat Sindbad's box?   ....

    h wants to sell Sindbad's goods?   ....

After you read

14 Work with two other students. Have this conversation.

    Student A: You are Sindbad. You are in the giant's house with your friends. You want to get away. Tell your friends about your plan.

    Student B: You are another merchant. You don't think this is a good plan. You don't want to try it. Say why.

    Student C: You are another merchant. You think it is a very good idea. You want your friend to help. Say why.

The Fourth Voyage

Before you read

15 Discuss these questions: Would you like to be Sindbad? Would you like to go on his voyages? Why (not)?

16 Who says or thinks these words?

    a 'This is my last hour.' ....

    b 'I want you to marry.' ....

    c 'In this country a man has to follow his
dead wife.' ....

    d 'I cannot change the ways of my country.' ....

    e 'I am not from this country, so it is different
for me.' ....

    f 'That was my last voyage!' ....

After you read

17 What happens to Sindbad after his wife dies? Why? Tell the story.

The Fifth Voyage

Before you read

18 Look at the picture on page 26. What can you see? What is happening?

While you read

19 Finish each sentence. Write one word.

    a Sindbad's friends find a giant bird's ....

    b They break the egg with big ....

    c They eat the .... bird.

    d The sky goes .... when the parent birds fly over.

    e The .... carry big, heavy stones.

    f One of the stones falls on Sindbad's ....

    g The wind carries Sindbad to an ....

    h The old man pushes and .... Sindbad.

    i After the old man drinks wine, Sindbad .... him to
the ground.

    j Sindbad throws stones at the monkeys and the monkeys throw
down ....

20 Work with another student. Have this conversation.

    Student A: You are Sindbad. You are home again and you want to sell your wood to a friend. Answer his questions.

    Student B: You are a merchant and Sindbad's friend. Ask him about his wood. How did he get it? Do you want to buy it?

The Sixth Voyage

Before you read

21 Sindbad sails to India on his sixth voyage. Discuss these questions.

    a What do you know about India?

    b What do you think Sindbad will find there?

While you read

22 Which is the right word in each sentence?

    a Sindbad goes to *cities / villages* in India.

    b The sea takes Sindbad's ship into a *cave / valley*.

    c Sindbad goes through it on *a boat / some wood*.

    d A *kind / angry* man speaks to Sindbad in Arabic.

    e Sindbad goes to the king's city on a *horse / ship*.

    f The King of Serendip is *kind / unkind* to Sindbad.

After you read

23 How does Sindbad feel in the cave after his ship hits the walls? What does he see and hear? What does he think? Tell the class.

The Seventh Voyage

Before you read

24 Look at the picture on page 37. What is Sindbad doing? Why do you think there are a lot of dead elephants?

25 How will Sindbad feel after his seven voyages? Will he want to go on other voyages? Why (not)? Discuss these questions.

While you read

26 Who do we read about in this voyage? Write ✓ or ✗.

    a Khalif Harun al-Rashid   .....

    b monkey-men   .....

    c King Serendip   .....

    d pirates   .....

    e Sindbad's wife   .....

    f the Old Man of the Sea   .....

    g elephants   .....

After you read

27 Sindbad shouts to the elephants, 'I understand you now!' What does he understand?

Writing

28 Write about one of Sindbad's voyages. Why was it dangerous? How did Sindbad get away? Was he clever, or did somebody help him?

29 Write about Sindbad's life in Baghdad. Is life better for him there or at sea?

30 You are one of the merchants at the Valley of Diamonds. You are an old man now and you are writing your life story. Write about Sindbad?

31 Write about a day in the life of Sindbad's wife.

32 You are a coconut merchant. Write a letter to a friend about your work. How do you get the coconuts? What do you do to them before you sell them? Where do you sell them?

33 Finish King Serendip's letter to the Khalif (in the Sixth Voyage).

34 Write a letter from a new friend in another country to Sindbad. What is happening in your country now? Will you see Sindbad again?

35 Look again at the map at the front of the book. Which place would you like to visit? Why?

WORD LIST

captain (n) The *captain* took the ship south to Argentina.

cave (n) The animals live in cold, dark *caves*.

coconut (n) The boy climbed the trees and threw down the *coconuts*.

diamond (n) When I'm rich, I shall wear *diamonds*.

elephant (n) We cut down the trees and then *elephants* carry them to the road.

giant (n/adj) He is a very big man – a *giant*!

goods (n pl) They buy *goods* in Poland and sell them in Russia.

hole (n) There is a *hole* in the door. One of the boys put his foot through it.

island (n) You can take a boat from here to the *islands*.

king (n) Please stand up before the *king* comes into the room.

merchant (n) *Merchants* brought coffee and tea from India to Europe.

monkey (n) *Monkeys* jumped from tree to tree.

pirate (n) *Pirates* climbed onto the ship and killed everybody.

saddle (n) I can't sit on a horse without a *saddle*.

sail (v) They are going to *sail* across the Atlantic to Miami.

snake (n) There were dangerous *snakes* under the house.

stone (n/adj) Do you build houses from wood or *stone*?

tusk (n) People kill elephants for their *tusks*.

valley (n) The village is in the *valley*, near the river.

voyage (n) The sea *voyage* from Britain to Egypt took weeks because we stopped on the way.

Treasure Island
Robert Louis Stevenson

A young boy, Jim Hawkins, lives quietly by the sea with his mother and father. One day, Billy Bones comes to live with them and from that day everything is different. Jim meets Long John Silver, a man with one leg, and Jim and Long John Silver go far across the sea in a ship called the *Hispaniola* to Treasure Island.

The Mummy

"Imhotep is half-dead and will be half-dead for all time."

The Mummy is an exciting movie. Imhotep dies in Ancient Egypt. 3,700 years later Rick O'Connell finds him. Imhotep is very dangerous. Can O'Connell send him back to the dead? *Based on the successful film*.

The Last of the Mohicans
James Fenimore Cooper

Uncas is the last of the Mohican Indians. He is with his father and Hawkeye when they meet Heyward. Heyward is taking the two young daughters of a British colonel to their father. But a Huron Indian who hates the British is near. Will the girls see their father again?

There are hundreds of Penguin Readers to choose from – world classics, film adaptations, modern-day crime and adventure, short stories, biographies, American classics, non-fiction, plays ...

For a complete list of all Penguin Readers titles, please contact your local Pearson Longman office or visit our website.

Jumanji

Jumanji is a strange and dangerous game. When someone throws the dice unusual things start to happen and the players must finish the game – before it finishes them. *Based on the thrilling film starring Robin Williams.*

Robinson Crusoe
Daniel Defoe

Robinson Crusoe is shipwrecked onto an island after a storm at sea. Are there other people? How will he survive? Will he be rescued? *A classic tale of survival based on a true story.*

Matilda
Roald Dahl

Matilda is a very clever little girl, but her terrible parents don't like her, and her head teacher, Miss Trunchbull, is very frightening. She isn't very happy. Then one day Matilda starts moving things with her eyes, and after that she isn't afraid of anybody! *Also a film starring Danny De Vito.*

There are hundreds of Penguin Readers to choose from – world classics, film adaptations, modern-day crime and adventure, short stories, biographies, American classics, non-fiction, plays ...

For a complete list of all Penguin Readers titles, please contact your local Pearson Longman office or visit our website.

www.penguinreaders.com

Pirates of the Caribbean
The Curse of the Black Pearl

Elizabeth lives on a Caribbean island, a very dangerous place. A young blacksmith is interested in her, but pirates are interested too. Where do the pirates come from and what do they want? Is there really a curse on their ship? And why can't they enjoy their gold?

Jaws
Peter Benchley

Amity is a quiet town near New York. One night a young woman goes for a swim in the sea. She doesn't come back. The next morning the police find her dead on the beach.

Brody is a good policeman, and he thinks there's a shark near Amity. He tries to close the beaches, but people won't listen to him. *A terrifying adventure and a popular film.*

Moby Dick
Herman Melville

Moby Dick is the most dangerous whale in the oceans. Captain Ahab fought him and lost a leg. Now he hates Moby Dick. He wants to kill him. But can Captain Ahab and his men find the great white whale? A young sailor, Ishmael, tells the story of their exciting and dangerous trip.

There are hundreds of Penguin Readers to choose from – world classics, film adaptations, modern-day crime and adventure, short stories, biographies, American classics, non-fiction, plays ...

For a complete list of all Penguin Readers titles, please contact your local Pearson Longman office or visit our website.

www.penguinreaders.com

Longman Dictionaries

Express yourself with confidence!

PEARSON
Longman

---

*Longman has led the way in ELT dictionaries since 1935.
We constantly talk to students and teachers around the
world to find out what they need from a learner's dictionary.*

Why choose a Longman dictionary?

Easy to understand

Longman invented the Defining Vocabulary – 2000 of the most
common words which are used to write the definitions in our
dictionaries. So Longman definitions are always clear and easy
to understand.

Real, natural English

All Longman dictionaries contain natural examples taken from
real-life that help explain the meaning of a word and show you
how to use it in context.

Avoid common mistakes

Longman dictionaries are written specially for learners, and we
make sure that you get all the help you need to avoid common
mistakes. We analyse typical learners' mistakes and include
notes on how to avoid them.

Innovative CD-ROMs

Longman are leaders in dictionary CD-ROM innovation. Did
you know that a dictionary CD-ROM includes features to help
improve your pronunciation, help you practice for exams and
improve your writing skills?

**For details of all Longman dictionaries, and to choose
the one that's right for you, visit our website:**

www.longman.com/dictionaries